Arts of the Islamic Book